AIR UNIVERSITY
AIR COMMAND AND STAFF COLLEGE

Holistic Debriefing

A Paradigm Shift in Leadership

ROLF FOLLAND
Lieutenant Colonel, Royal Norwegian Air Force

Air Command and Staff College
Wright Flyer Paper No. 41

Air University Press
Maxwell Air Force Base, Alabama

March 2010

This Wright Flyer Paper and others in the series are available electronically at the Air University Research Web site http://research.maxwell.af.mil and the AU Press Web site http://aupress.au.af.mil.

Disclaimer

Opinions, conclusions, and recommendations expressed or implied within are solely those of the author and do not necessarily represent the views of Air University, the United States Air Force, the Department of Defense, or any other US government agency. Cleared for public release: distribution unlimited.

Foreword

It is with great pride that Air Command and Staff College presents another in a series of award-winning student research projects from our academic programs that reach nearly 11,000 students each year. As our series title indicates, we seek to promote the sort of imaginative, forward-looking thinking that inspired the earliest aviation pioneers, and we aim for publication projects which combine these characteristics with the sort of clear presentation that permits even the most technical topics to be readily understood. We sincerely hope what follows will stimulate thinking, invite debate, and further encourage today's air war fighters in their continuing search for new and better ways to perform their missions—now and in the future.

ANTHONY J. ROCK
Brigadier General, USAF
Commandant

Abstract

From time to time, paradigm shifts occur in leadership in the sense that fundamental assumptions about the mechanisms of human performance change. We are currently undergoing a paradigm shift that might highlight transformational leadership as highly effective in the context of military operations. The reason is that transformational leadership facilitates the growth of motivational mechanisms when confronting extreme situations like war. In essence, military subordinates expect their leaders to have more interpersonal skills than were required before. This is partly a result of the shift in community wherein employers now are expected to take responsibility for individuals' lifelong personal growth and partly a result of increased stress due to higher demands in international operations.

This paper explores the utility of a debriefing method resulting in individual, unit, and organizational transcendence toward increased effectiveness in the Royal Norwegian Air Force (RNoAF). The conceptual framework is centered on the transformational and complexity theories of leadership science. The study offers for consideration a debriefing methodology termed "holistic" as a structure for achieving both individualistic and unit inner growth and efficiency. The problem examined is the lack of proper leadership tools in the RNoAF's operational units to understand and cope with the effects of increased stress. Based on theory and examples from operational practice, holistic debriefing is presented as a possible means for leaders to increase mission effectiveness through improved stress coping mechanisms. The secondary effects from people engaging with themselves and each other through holistic debriefing are increased self-knowledge, interpersonal trust, group confidence, and an improved working environment.

Preface

In the last eight years I have been a leader for combat helicopter units in the Royal Norwegian Air Force. I have served as a squadron commander twice, once at the Norwegian Coast Guard helicopter squadron and a second tour as commander of the Norwegian search and rescue helicopter squadron. In both situations I was responsible for a 24-hour-a-day, 365-day-a-year response capability in which the crew members had to be capable of performing lifesaving missions under extreme conditions. Several experiences from these missions and their follow-on debriefings have made me question our concepts of learning. As the years passed, it seemed obvious to me that a hidden potential of growth and development exists in the questions we never asked—the questions that dealt with our emotional experiences. I like to view it as the invisible part of an "iceberg of information"—we know it is there, but we do not dive into the cold water to have a closer look.

In 2001 I decided to initiate a new form of debriefing to address the hidden part of the "iceberg." At that time we called it *psychological debriefing* because we used the same procedures to debrief traumatic events. As time went on we decided to integrate the emotional aspect into the regular debriefing. The title has evolved to *holistic debriefing* because this method integrates all relevant aspects of the learning process—cognitional, behavioral, and emotional—and better represents the intent of the debriefing style. The effects of this holistic approach exceeded all our expectations. First, I witnessed strengthened relations and a more open atmosphere among colleagues. Moreover, I received feedback from my flight commanders that several crew members actually functioned better in their roles on the aircraft. A concept that initially started as an experiment proved to have an operational value of improved mission effectiveness.

I wish to recognize the inspiration, assistance, and support of several individuals and groups who have helped me in the development of holistic debriefing and the preparation of this research paper. First, I owe a special debt of gratitude to the Royal Norwegian Air Force, which accepts innovative thinking and has given me the freedom to try this new concept of debriefing. Second, I'd like to thank my friend and instructor at the Norwegian Air War Academy, Lt Col Ole Asbjorn Solberg, for supporting and guiding me through the implementation of psychological debriefing into the 330th Squadron. Third, I'd like to thank the personnel at the 330th and 337th Squadrons for being open to innovation, change, and development and having trust in the concept. Finally, I'd like to thank my course instructor at Air Command and Staff College, Lt Col Brian W. Landry, for his enthusiasm in guiding me through the process that resulted in this paper.

Introduction

One search and rescue (SAR) mission in the northern part of Norway in July 2000 gave me new insight in how the negative effect of stress can have a devastating impact on performance. We had first been scrambled on a car accident with several injured children. After having landed the helicopter on the road, we tried to save the four young siblings who were thrown out of the wrecked car. It was a terrible scene. We did our best, but only one of the children survived. When we were about to hand over the child to the hospital, we got another mission. A 17-year-old girl was missing after a class excursion in the mountains nearby. The weather was perfect, with blue skies, and the terrain was clearly set out with grass-grown hills. The girl was dressed in a white T-shirt and red trousers. This should be an easy task. After three fuel loads we still could not find her. A search patrol on the ground found her some hours later. She told them that we had flown over her at least 20 times while she was waving with her white T-shirt. Six professional SAR crew members had not seen her. Why?

—Sea King pilot in command
Royal Norwegian Air Force (RNoAF) SAR
helicopter, Banak Air Station, Norway

Emotions have for a long time been a neglected area in civilian as well as military leadership. Few researchers have focused on the emotional aspect of leadership, and literature related to leadership has given very little attention to them. Leadership has been dominated by a cognitive focus wherein emotions have been viewed as a negative element for rationality and efficiency. In the 1990s, the emotional element in leadership was the subject of growing interest and focus. As an example, Bernard Bass introduced the term *transformational leadership*, in which the emotional aspect has important significance for effective leadership.[1] In transformational leadership, the leader influences the followers through an emotional connection involving trust, admiration, and respect. But leadership is also a rational process in which mutual cooperation is assumed between the leader and the follower. Thus, the leader is also a team player. A team is better conditioned for success when its members experience a feeling of mutual trust, openness, and respect. And when team members exchange emotional experiences, stronger attachment and mutual connection develop that break down anonymity. Effective leadership can therefore be viewed as resulting from the leader's ability to integrate the emotional aspect in relation to the followers to achieve mission effectiveness.

Debriefing, in the traditional military context, has been used to analyze the mission to increase effectiveness by gaining experience through behavioral and cognitive learning. An emphasis on these aspects will amplify operational learning and improved tactical knowledge and skills. But learning is more than just an accumulation of knowledge. It is learning that causes a change in an individual's behavior in the manner of dealing with things that the individual chooses in the future and the individual's opinions and personality. Learning involves change in one form or another: either the inner, experience-based level or in the external behavior that can be observed by others.[2] Therefore, since it is difficult to imagine emotionless human behavior and cognition, the traditional debriefing is insufficient. Stressors like high-risk missions and accidents involve strong emotional and physiological activation, and if the emotional activation and experience are not included in the debriefing, valuable knowledge can be lost and stress may accumulate. Because of this, mission effectiveness may be degraded.

> *After the accident I experienced nightmares. I was always on the same approach for landing, but the outcome could vary. Some nights I handled the situation well, other nights I crashed and burned. But it was not only the nightmares that were difficult. In connection with approaches for landing I experienced discomfort, especially with corresponding weather conditions. I felt my reputation as a good pilot was weakened and was afraid of situations where I once again could fail. My self-confidence*

> *[was] reduced to a level that made me avoid challenging situations at work. And I did not even discuss the problems with my wife. On the contrary, I got annoyed by comments about the accident and fled away from the difficulties instead of facing them.*
>
> —Norwegian F-16 pilot
> Moldjord et al., *Liv og lære i operative miljøer*

Emotions have often been perceived as negative since they are often associated with a lack of control and difficulties with learning.[3] Jerome Bruner introduced an optimal learning process with the integration of three aspects: behavior, cognition, and emotion.[4] This process is useful when establishing a holistic approach for debriefing in the modern military unit. Individual emotions experienced before, during, or after the mission may or may not have an impact on the operational effectiveness of the group.

Communication of emotions is often difficult and is dependent on the level of trust and confidence established within the unit. It is the leader's responsibility to establish a sufficient level of trust and confidence, and it is therefore necessary to focus on the emotional and relational aspects in leadership training. Military leaders are responsible for the effective use of available resources to accomplish quality missions in hostile environments. Personnel are their most important resource, and mission effectiveness is dependent on individual maturity and knowledge. Using a more holistic debriefing, the military leader can build trust and confidence to a level that makes growth and development possible. The result can be increased mission effectiveness in a robust working environment characterized by openness, confidence, and mutual respect.

This study explores the benefits of holistic debriefing as a method of individual, unit, and organizational transcendence toward increased effectiveness in the RNoAF. It is presented in the context of the transformational and complexity theories of leadership science. This work offers for consideration a methodology termed *holistic debriefing* as a way of achieving both individualistic and unit inner growth and efficiency. The problem examined is the lack of proper tools given leaders in the RNoAF's operational units to understand and cope with the effects of increased stress. This study also examines holistic debriefing as a possible solution for leaders to mitigate the threat to operational personnel exposed to cumulative stress by creating a process for sharing experienced stressors valid for learning, including the emotional elements.

Debriefing: Old versus New

In traditional military debriefing, the focus has been reflection on the behavioral and cognitive aspects to provide the opportunity to review how the mission was conducted regarding procedures and tactics. It takes place through a structured dialogue between colleagues in a unit after a mission and is often led by the mission commander. Holistic debriefing addresses the emotional, cognitional, and behavioral aspects of military missions. By utilizing the psychological debriefing model Stress and Its Mastery as a framework to understand the emotional aspect of individual reactions, holistic debriefing integrates the emotional aspect in the traditional debriefing within a structured dialogue.[5] While the traditional debriefing focuses on facts and action in relation to procedures and tactics, the holistic debriefing integrates facts and action in relation to emotional tension experienced by the individual. The essence of holistic debriefing in a military context is improvement of individual self-knowledge and interpersonal trust through effective integration of behavior, cognition, and emotional aspects to a level that makes further growth and development possible.[6] The ultimate goal of incorporating holistic debriefing in the RNoAF is to increase mission effectiveness.

Significance of Debriefing

The Royal Norwegian Air Force has recognized the leaders of the organization—its officers—as the key. Leaders constantly have to balance shortfalls because there is never enough time, money, or manpower to accomplish the missions with guaranteed success. It is therefore important for military leaders to understand and develop both themselves and those under their command to meet the challenges with confidence and robustness. Leadership training is one of the most important means available for the organization to achieve exactly that. The chief of the Norwegian Defence Staff stated that "leadership training through personal development is the starting point for leaders who are responsible for individuals' performance in a stressful environment."[7] Furthermore, he has stated that the development of leaders and the exercising of leadership must go hand in hand and be a part of normal operations.[8] The chief of the Norwegian Defence Staff's approach to leadership emphasizes that military leaders must be able to lead their people in life-or-death combat situations. Therefore, in peacetime, leaders must train and develop personnel to create combat-ready units and functionally efficient staffs.[9] This sets clear guidance for the armed forces' training plans. Training in the management of crisis and combat, using learning by experience under guidance, is a declared area of emphasis.[10] In times of great transition and change, the situation demands not only more leadership but also newer forms of leadership.[11] A holistic view of human performance is one step toward this goal.

Since 1990 the amount of risk and stress for operational personnel in the RNoAF has increased due to a step-up in international engagement and higher demands for efficiency. Several aircrews have experienced the emotions related to the fear of death. Norwegian pilots have bombed live targets in Afghanistan. The tempo and intensity of and requirements for training and exercises have increased. At the same time, there have been political demands for workforce reduction and increased focus on financial management. The RNoAF has fulfilled the operational requirements, but the signs of negative effects are present. "Pilots are applying for the War Academy because they need some rest from the operational environment. The maintenance personnel resign due to stress. Officers are advertising for a better care-taking system after a traumatic event."[12] Therefore, the RNoAF is focusing on tools that can help the organization to sustain its proficiency in this "new" reality and thereby maintain itself as an attractive future employer and effective contributor of airpower.

Emotional debriefing has been used as a supplement to the traditional debriefing in two RNoAF squadrons since 2001, and the positive effects have raised the question of whether this concept can be integrated into the entire organization. Will the integration of emotional aspects in the traditional debriefing help leaders increase mission effectiveness in operational units and mitigate stress? First of all, this depends on the leader's confidence in bringing emotions to the surface within the unit. A sufficient confidence level can only be reached through education and practice in a safe environment, and it is crucial that the perception of insufficiency and failures in the training period do not lead to resistance and rejection later in the leader's career.

Holistic View on Debriefing

> *After the near-miss I started to back off. I was no longer the first one to volunteer for the difficult missions. I felt both anxiety and shame. Me—the best, toughest and roughest pilot in the squadron. . . . And since I did not manage to talk about it to the other pilots in the squadron the tension grew inside me. I only did it worse.*
>
> —Norwegian F-16 pilot
> Moldjord et al., *Liv og lære i operative miljøer*

This section explores the emotional aspects of our personality and their central function in regard to cognition and behavior in the professional arena. Specifically, it focuses on the existence of emotions and their functions in addition to the cognitional and behavioral elements. Jerome Bruner, an American psychologist and one of the principal architects of the cognitive revolution and educational reform in the United States and Great Britain in the second half of the twentieth century, argues that there is a close connection between cognition, emotion, and behavior in the human mind.[13] David Krech uses the expression *perfink*, which means that people perceive, feel, and think at the same time.[14] Bruner claims that they also act as a result of what they perfink and that the three elements have to be viewed in a holistic manner. He posits that "we can abstract each of these functions from the unified whole, but if we do so too rigidly we lose sight of the fact that it is one of the functions of a culture to keep them related and together in those images, stories, and the like by which our experience is given coherence and cultural relevance."[15] It can be fruitful to pursue the linkages between cognition, emotion, and behavior when designing a tool for learning from experience and reflection, and the military debriefing is meant to be such a tool. Its function is to improve mission effectiveness through a strengthened learning process of reflection on past performance. The problem is that the traditional debriefing is not balanced in relation to Bruner's "tripartism" because the emotional aspect is not given enough attention, if any at all. In other words, we do not reflect on what and how we were feeling as we executed the mission.

Bruner's classical triad visualizes the learning process consisting of action, cognition, and emotion, as depicted in figure 1. This can be expressed as a learning process wherein the three human operative systems are fully integrated into the learning environment. The components of behavior—emotion, cognition, and action—are not isolated from each other but are aspects of a larger whole that achieves its integration only within a cultural system.[16] Furthermore, Bruner claims that emotion should not be isolated from the knowledge of the situation that arouses it and that action is a final common path based on what one both knows and feels. It is important to recognize that "all three terms represent abstractions."[17] They are constructions

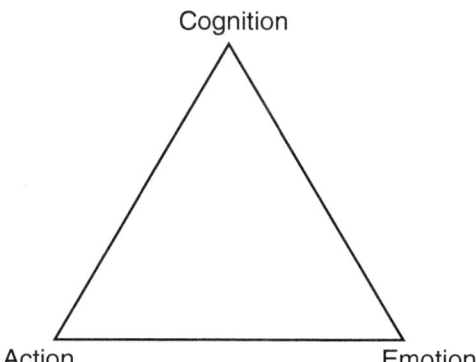

Figure 1. A visual picture of Bruner's triad. (*Adapted from* J. Bruner, *Actual Minds, Possible Worlds* [Cambridge, MA: Harvard University Press, 1986], 61.)

that are structurally independent and constitute a unified whole in our personality. *Personality* can be defined as "the characteristic patterns of behavior, thought, and emotion that determine a person's adjustment to the environment."[18]

The reason for focusing on emotion is the perception that feelings, emotion, or affection tends to live in the shadow of cognition and action in the military environment. Military personnel are traditionally trained to base their analyses, decisions, and interactions on cognition, with minimum influence from emotion. Emotions and feelings are traditionally viewed as signs of weakness in the professional military environment. The importance of emotional and relational aspects in human interaction, both in war and peace, can therefore be viewed as underestimated in the military environment. Misjudgment of the situation, suboptimal decision making, and difficult interaction can, in this context, be seen as a result of inadequate knowledge and/or acceptance of the emotional aspects in human interaction. Stress is a matter of regulating emotions, and the same mechanisms can therefore be present when coping with stress.

Stress

Stress is influential on holistic debriefing along two lines. First, sharing emotional aspects in a group can be stressful by itself. Second, sharing emotional experiences can be a relief valve that mitigates stress. Both aspects are important when integrating emotional aspects in the traditional debriefing and are discussed in this section.

The precondition for growth is the will and ability to challenge established structures and, thereby, security. Through holistic debriefing, one gets the chance to challenge existing self-knowledge in spite of insecurity and anxiety. Erich Fromm asserts that man's internal strength depends to a large extent on the truth about his real self.[19] But such training can be hard, and the truth about oneself can be too tough for the individual. Carl Rogers asserts that personal learning involves a good deal of pain and anxiety. And according to Paul Moxnes, "the word anxiety contains a meaning that is very similar to the term *insecurity*."[20] However, Søren Kierkegaard describes anxiety as "the possibility of freedom, where life is a synthesis between what is given and what we can choose." Nevertheless, standing face-to-face with the opportunity to choose may be a frightening experience because freedom to choose may involve endless consequences. Kierkegaard articulates that "anxiety is an experience of the possibility of freedom. It is only by relating to ourselves that we are in a position to undertake an existential choice."[21] Moxnes claims that "anxiety is an experience, and how the situation is perceived is the critical factor for anxiety, not how real the actual danger is."[22] In other words, anxiety is the object of perceptual interpretation. From this perspective, participants in holistic debriefing could experience different degrees of anxiety, and some will not experience any anxiety at all. Many factors can influence this, including the individual's self-perception, previous experience, motivation, and so on. Thus, participants will have differing suppositions regarding the activities to be undertaken, and they will have differing perceptions of whatever it is they will be attempting to do. Anxiety arises when there is lack of congruence between a person's self-perception and the new experiences to be undertaken. Steinar Bjartveit and Trond Kjærstad posited that anxiety can express itself as "a vague, uncomfortable feeling where one perceives oneself as insecure, tense, and helpless."[23]

In spite of this potential insecurity and anxiety about the unknown, the assumption is that the personnel will participate in holistic debriefing to undergo new experiences that contribute to development. The challenge in relation to self-development consists of finding the optimal level of security for each individual, that is to say, a level of stress sufficient to motivate growth.

Stress, Panic, and Performance

There is energy in stress, and this is often the source of motivation and improved performance.[24] The problem is, if stress becomes too powerful, it destroys motivation and worsens performance. The Panic and Performance Model, developed by Michael Useem, shows the basic relationship between stress and performance (see fig. 2). The key point about the curve is the "panic point" where the performance level is at its highest. To the right of the panic point, the performance level will decrease rapidly due to overwhelm-

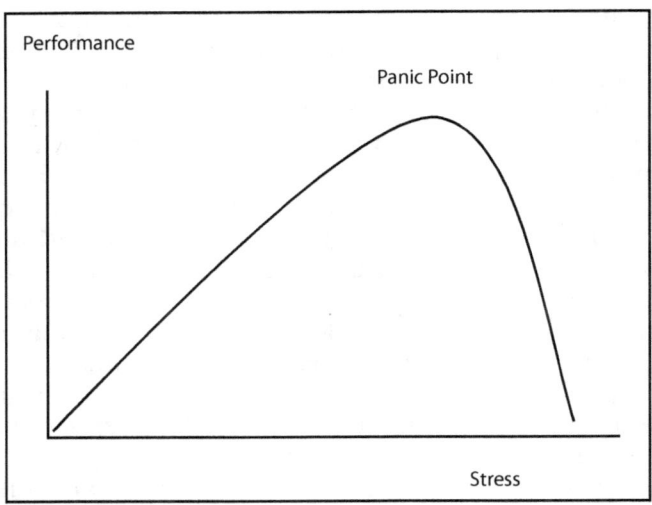

Figure 2. Panic and Performance Model. (*Adapted from* M. Useem, *The Leadership Moment: Nine True Stories of Triumph and Disaster and Their Lessons for Us All* [New York: Three Rivers Press, 1998].)

ing stress. According to Useem, "psychologists tell us that panic sets in when the mind succumbs to stress and fails to take in new information about a threatening event, or fails for similar reasons to take advantage of prior experience germane to the threat."[25] Nevertheless, the object should never be to remove stress but to build up the confidence necessary to reduce stress to an acceptable level.[26] A leader should therefore want stress to remain at a level that makes growth and development possible. Kierkegaard analyzed Abraham's willingness to sacrifice Isaac to show that through experiencing stress one will experience growth in the strength of the self.[27] The self and its security are strengthened by saying yes to challenging one's fears. In this way stress facilitates positive development.

Coping with Stress

One assumption is that holistic debriefing allows personnel to access the skills needed to cope with stress simply by establishing a dialogue that does not stigmatize emotions in military activity. After all, everyone experiences stress, and there is little stigma attached to improving coping skills in the military organization. For example, some military personnel are suffering the effects of post-traumatic stress disorder and are forced to leave the military because of their inability to cope. Historically, the professional military environment has not been able to meet the psychological or emotional impact of combat with the same seriousness as it meets physical injury. Emotional disorder has been labeled as cowardice, desertion, and lack of moral fiber. The cause of the problem has been isolated to the individual's inability to cope with stress. However, it is more likely that the cause is the accuser's own inability to deal with the stigmatized emotional aspect. Certainly, some individuals are more vulnerable than others. But modern military organizations are investing more and more resources in each individual for specialization and professionalism, and it is not efficient to prevent highly skilled personnel from achieving their potential because of organizational inability to cope with the negative effects of stress. It is much easier to create an environment that gives individuals the ability to bring their emotional experiences to the surface among colleagues to prevent stress accumulation. Inasmuch as stress arises from the interaction between the person and the environment, stress management may require both organizational and personal change.[28] The strength of holistic debriefing lies in its flexibility. It gives the leader the ability to respond both to the requirements of the organization and to personal needs. Through holistic debriefing, personnel can learn new skills, either in self or others, and the organization can establish a strong connection to the individual.

Individual's Needs and Tendencies

Holistic debriefing can be a tool for learning more about "the unknown self." Part of the reason for this rests in fundamental human needs.[29] Abraham Maslow describes the need for self-realization as the only need that, in principle, cannot be satisfied.[30] The most important aspect of Maslow's theory is that it points out the need for growth and development. Learning that involves a change in self-understanding and self-perception is threatening and can lead to opposition and defensive reactions in some people. Giving up one's defensive behavior and thereby broadening one's horizons are often difficult for an individual. This is why it has to be accomplished under conditions hallmarked by trust and confidence.

Moxnes describes two fundamental levels of needs, primary needs and secondary needs, which contain dimensions that may be seen as contradictory. *Primary needs* concern security and growth. On one hand, man is driven to seek *security*. We flee from dangerous and threatening situations, resist change, and oppose new learning. On the other hand, *growth* is influenced by man's curiosity, which leads him to seek excitement in his life and drives him toward the maximization of achievement. Moxnes claims that "these two needs are to be found in every person, and they conflict with one another."[31] In essence, growth is usually at the expense of security, and contrarily, when man seeks security, it is usually at the expense of growth.

Secondary needs relate to the need for control (meaning) and freedom. Man's need for *meaning* and *control* means we seek values and norms; we want order and system. At the same time, we have a need for *freedom* and the ability to choose. We desire to stretch our boundaries with the fewest possible restrictions.[32] These two secondary needs are more concrete than primary needs. Moxnes articulates that "a desire for freedom indicates an underlying growth need, and a quest after meaning expresses an underlying security need."[33]

In addition to primary and secondary needs, *two fundamental tendencies*, courage and fear, are found in most people. On the one hand is the tendency toward courage or heroism. On the other is the tendency toward fear or cowardice. Moxnes states that "these two tendencies can be present in one and the same individual, and they will mutually try to exclude one another." *Courage* is hallmarked by people being persistent, being willing to take risks, and thus being willing to take the consequences that follow from that. The consequences of *fear* are that people stay within themselves and withdraw. We want to preserve what we are used to and what we feel safe with. Thus, we shy away from the possibility of freedom and growth. Courage and fear are not needs but tendencies that follow man through his life. Moxnes claims that "people can change from the one tendency to the other, but when they do so they also change personality."³⁴ Traumatic experiences can make people change their personality, and one can assume that powerful mental stressors experienced in extremely uncertain situations can create a personal crisis. Prolonged exposure to the environment of war will affect a person's feelings and reactions in some way. Unofficial surveys indicate that the divorce rate among Norwegian military officers with multiple deployments is as high as 70 percent.³⁵ The US Army reports suicide rates among active-duty soldiers to be at an all-time high since it started tracking soldier suicide rates in 1980.³⁶ The numbers indicate two important aspects for any military commander in war. First, military organizations in war are morally obligated to develop systems and procedures that can mitigate long-term negative effects on personnel. In addition, the numbers indicate that our current systems and tools are not sufficient.

War challenges an individual's primary and secondary needs because of its uncertain and brutal nature. Thus, it is crucial for military personnel to understand the emotional impact of traumatic events and to therefore develop a secure collegial arena where experiences can be shared and diffused. Growth, freedom, and courage are dimensions that relate to holistic debriefing. The assumption is that most personnel will consciously seek growth in spite of the prospect of increased fear, reduced meaning, and deficient security. These dimensions create a fundamental starting point in the person. According to Moxnes, "the question becomes simply to what extent one can teach oneself to know oneself, how painful this will be, and what consequences it will have."³⁷

Learning and Transfer of Learning

The purpose of the military debriefing is to filter the most important elements from the mission for learning and growth so that the next mission can be performed with higher proficiency. It is a common perception that learning has to do with change. Carl Rogers said that meaningful learning is that which is more than just an accumulation of knowledge. "It is learning that causes a change in an individual's behavior, in the manner of dealing with things that the individual chooses in the future and in the individual's opinions and personality. Learning involves change in one form or another, either at the inner, experience-based level or in external behavior that can be observed by others."[38]

Transfer of learning is a very important problem in educational theory.[39] The question is whether what one discovers in debriefing is transferable to operational performance. Moxnes says that transfer of learning often has its limits. Methods such as sensitivity training seem to have great meaning for the individual participant in the short term but have little effect on the organizational productivity in the long term.[40] These training programs have often been short-lived and taken place in an unfamiliar environment that makes it difficult to transfer the learning back to the work environment. Viewed against this potential pitfall, holistic debriefing can offer an easier way to transfer new individual insight from the debriefing process to the performance of the next mission. Holistic debriefing builds on and expands from the traditional debriefing well-known to all airmen, and the basic security necessary for learning is therefore already established. Furthermore, the emotional part of the debriefing will always build on trust, willingness, and the individual's ability to adapt. The core of the concept is that the group decides how fast and how deep the emotional process shall progress—not the leader. Individual drive for growth must come from within, and it is the individual who must transfer new insight from theory to practice. However, the fact that the process is open will secure common insight, and relations within the group will aid individual learning to occur in practice.

The Psychodynamic Model

The human mind is complex and diffuse, and a common model for simplification is necessary to make the journey toward better understanding possible in the military working environment. Holistic debriefing is a structured dialogue in which the purpose is to bring all potential learning aspects of a certain situation to the surface, including the emotional aspect. Several conditions have to be present for individuals to share emotional and often diffuse experiences with colleagues. The key words are *trust* and *confi-*

dence. The individual must feel that colleagues will listen openly and try to understand the shared information in a constructive context. This requires a common language and a shared reference point. The primary premise for a successful holistic debriefing is to work on a basic level with tools that make our behavior and actions understandable. Bruner's classical triad represents an example of a basic visual picture of personality, wherein the balance between the three human operative systems forms the personality and the individual's behavior. Nevertheless, one premise in this kind of debriefing is to establish a common understanding of some central mechanisms for human behavior. One central aspect in this context is the protecting layer between our inner feelings and our visible behavior.

In psychodynamic literature, different labels are used for the concept of the human core. E. Tory Higgins labels the human core as "the actual self."[41] Other terms are Donald Winnicott's "the true self," Frode Nyeng's "the authentically human," Nina Monsen's "the loving human," John Pierrakos's "the higher self," and so on.[42] All these names call attention to the essence of holistic debriefing: a proper balance between cognition, action, and emotion *in* the individual and *between* the individual and the situation he or she is facing.

Higgins is indicating three self-conditions: "the actual self," the attributes believed to be possessed by an individual; "the ideal self," the attributes an individual would like to possess; and "the ought self," the attributes an individual believes he should possess. Furthermore, he outlines two types of standpoints on the individual self: one's own personal standpoint and the standpoint of a significant other (for example, a colleague). According to Higgins, when discrepancies involve the self and standpoints on the self, emotional tensions can be heightened (anxiety and stress).[43]

Different development programs within the RNoAF have used Joar Skjevdal's Core Model as a basic tool for analysis and understanding of the human core (see fig. 3). This is an idealistic model of the human being where different layers or elements form the total "self."[44] Skjevdal suggests that the Core Model contributes to a common language on the inner journey for better understanding oneself in relationship with others.[45] In this way, the model provides the foundation for the collegial relationship in holistic debriefing.

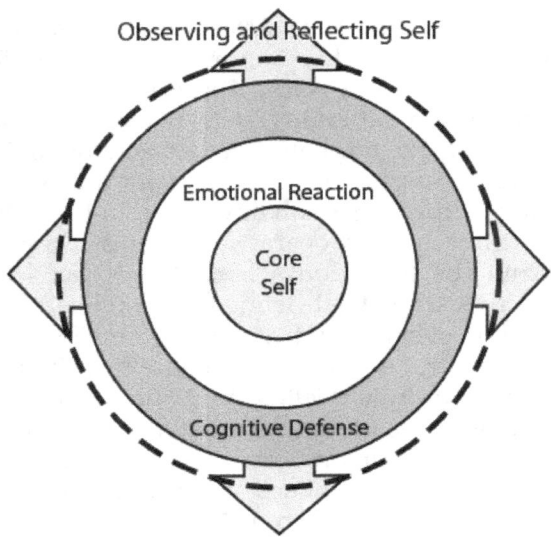

Figure 3. The Core Model. (Reproduced and simplified with permission from Joar Skjevdal, AFF Consulting, Oslo, Norway. See C. Moldjord, A. Arntzen, K. Firing, O. A. Solberg, and J. C. Laberg, *Liv og lære i operative miljøer. Tøffe menn grater!* [Bergen, Norway: Fagbokforlaget, 2007], 369.)

The basic assumption is that the natural core self first of all wants to relate to the environment with sufficient openness, acceptance, and trust for safe self-actualization. The two fundamental sources for human motivation—the need for appreciation and development—work in mutual dependence in real life. The drive for development is dependent on sufficient openness, acceptance, and trust.[46] This idea complements Higgins's self-discrepancy theory. First, self-discrepancy theory assumes people are motivated to reach a condition in which their self-concept matches their personally relevant self-guides; and second, relations between and among different types of self-state representations represent different kinds of psychological situations, which in turn are associated with distinct emotional-motivational states.[47]

Some people do not have a large discrepancy between their actual self-conception and their ideal self. These people are presumed to be more motivated and to have greater self-esteem. The individual illustrated in the ideal Core Model is a person with an accessible core self and a growing observing and reflecting self characterized by empathy, understanding, and boundary setting for oneself and the environment.[48] With flexibility, individuals can use their innate ability for openness, intellectual development, creativity, trust, vitality, empathy, care, and energy, depending on the situation. This is fundamental to the individual's ability to regulate emotions and cope with stress. When these qualities are present, the individual has a healthy capacity for self-regulation because of highly developed self-knowledge. The holistic debriefing can be a valuable tool to build a better capacity for self-regulation. Increased ability to regulate emotions and cope with stress will increase mission effectiveness because each individual will be able to meet the challenges with more mental robustness and colleagues will be able to understand the individual's reactions in a more constructive way.

The Holistic Debriefing Model

The Stress and Its Mastery Model (fig. 4) is taken from the RNoAF Academy's manual *Emotional Debriefing*.[49] This model creates a clear framework for understanding the individual effects of stress and the resulting stress reactions and has mainly been used for debriefing traumatic events.

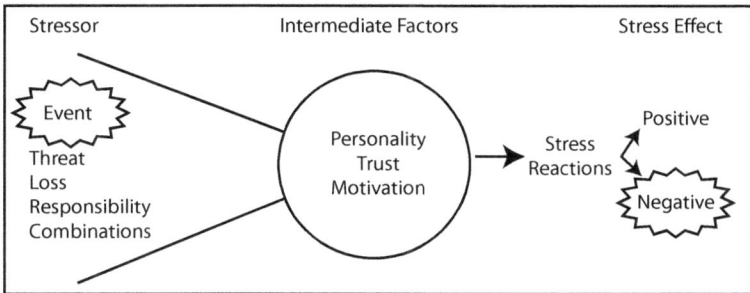

Figure 4. Stress and Its Mastery Model. (*Adapted from* Ole A. Solberg, *Krisehaandtering—Emosjonell Debriefing* [Emotional Debriefing], a compendium at Norwegian Air War Academy [Trondheim, Norway: Luftkrigsskolen, 1997].)

The model visualizes some of the mechanisms in play when a person experiences stressful events and can therefore be a viable tool when establishing a structured approach for holistic debriefing. The intent is to integrate the emotional aspect into the traditional debriefing with an understandable structure. This model represents a visualization of the framework used in psychological debriefing in the RNoAF's 330th and 337th Squadrons in the period 2001–2007. This model illustrates that the effect of stressors is modified by intermediate variables like personality factors, trust, and motivation and that stress reactions are the result of interplay between stressors and intermediate variables. In reality the concepts are far more complex.

Stress has traditionally been used as a collective concept with a large degree of subjectivity and is measureable only to a limited extent. In the context of holistic debriefing, stress is regarded as experienced emotional reactions within the individual and the unit. Karsten Hytten and Holger Ursin label a stressor as "external loads on the organism."[50] This can be present as a psychosocial threat. Psychosocial threats can be further divided into "threats to others' lives," "threats to social values and the values of others," "the stress of responsibility," and "the fear of making mistakes."[51] The intensity of the stress and its effect on the individual seem to be dependent upon proximity to the event, exposure time, and distance from the centre of the event.[52] The stressor becomes overwhelming when it jerks individuals out of their normal equilibrium and when the external event represents a threat to people's fundamental values.[53] The stressor concept used in the holistic debriefing relates to Hytten and Ursin's definition and is viewed as "external stimuli that represent a potential burden." In the holistic debriefing the stressor is detected by focusing on facts and perception by answering the question *what happened?* The key is to create a common understanding of the entire situation. Typical follow-up questions are *where did it happen, what was said,* and *what made you react?*

Individuals measure or filter stress through several mechanisms. In the debriefing process the intermediate variables are detected and analyzed through asking the questions *what did you hear, what did you see, what did you think, and what did you feel?* The key in this phase is to understand the background or framework for decisions and actions that have been made, including the sense impressions that had a potential impact on the individual's judgments. This is then followed up with the question *how did you react?* The purpose is to integrate the emotional aspects with the cognitive and behavioral aspects to create a better understanding and normalization of the individual's reactions and behavior.

Initially, it is recommended to establish a basic structure of variables when integrating emotional aspects in the debriefing process. The assumption is that this will help the participants avoid an amorphous discussion that confuses the process. As the concept of holistic debriefing becomes more integrated into the unit's regular debriefing, the structure should be looser. The structured elements used in the psychological debriefing initiated in the two maritime RNoAF helicopter squadrons have been personality factors, motivation, and trust. These variables are valuable in holistic debriefing because they seem to be important when trying to understand human growth and development.

Personality Factors

Most definitions of personality build upon the assumption that the individual's characteristics remain fairly stable over time. Gordon Allport viewed personality as "the dynamic organization within the individual of those psychophysical systems that determine his unique adjustments to his environment."[54] This definition represents a holistic dynamic perspective. Psychologists do not agree on the degree of consistency in personality, but most agree that people are predisposed to act in certain ways based on individual characteristics and situational conditions. If we as military leaders are interested in effecting change, growth, and development, it is vital to focus on developing greater individual self-knowledge as well as knowledge of each other within the unit. In her book *Leadership and the New Science*, Margaret Wheatley claims that if we want to bring health to a system, we must "connect it more to itself." She says that "the system needs to learn more about itself from itself." This applies to the individual as well as to the organization. Furthermore, Wheatley asserts that "the system needs processes to bring it together."[55]

Holistic debriefing can be the process or framework that establishes an arena for officers to connect, develop relationships, and learn how to better cope with stress based on new insight. By using the framework of emotional debriefing, visualized in the model Stress and Its Mastery, holistic debriefing can contribute to increased self-awareness. By establishing a cognitive map and offering time for reflection in small groups, holistic debriefing can be a way for the leader to help subordinates understand their personal characteristics and mechanisms that make them behave in a certain way. The new insight may lead to change if the individual is motivated.

One of the respondents in a survey that asked about the perceived effects of psychological debriefing at the RNoAF's 337th Squadron observed that "many of the flight safety initiatives, the way we debrief and interact with each other, lead to increased self-knowledge. Self-knowledge makes it easier to understand a colleague's situation—and thereby we have increased empathy and trust within the unit.[56] Several of the respondents from the RNoAF's 330th and 337th Squadrons reported a perceived improvement in the working environment together with leaders who have become more focused on both the operational and emotional aspects of daily operations.[57]

Motivation

Motivation for lasting individual change is not in response to a leader's demands or wishes. For a change to be more than transitory, the motivation has to come from the individual. The concept of motivation comes from the Latin *movere*, which means "to set in motion." It can be viewed as a force that makes a person take action in a particular way and drives the person toward achieving something. Motivation is connected to emotion, since a driving feeling starts off or creates a physical action. And as Moxnes describes, the individual's primary (security and growth) and secondary (meaning and freedom) needs are fundamental to that individual. Since new insight in all three aspects of Bruner's triad is the central factor in holistic debriefing, the creation of an environment able to meet the individual's primary and secondary needs is crucial for success.

Motivation, in the holistic debriefing context, is related to the individual's wish and desire to be more effective through personal growth and development. The assumption is that by engaging together to learn more about themselves, people tend to establish strong relations and a collective identity that lead to increased motivation for improvement. The experiences after introducing psychological debriefing to the RNoAF's 330th and 337th Squadrons indicate this assumption is right. One subjective example of this is the author's personal experience as a pilot in command on a SAR mission where 12 Icelandic fishermen were about to be crushed against the North Cape during a hard winter storm:

> The weather was terrible with heavy snowfall and gusts of 50 knots. It was night and total darkness. But we had a job to do. As we lifted off, everything seemed to be fine. But five minutes after takeoff, the winds changed direction and increased due to the Venturi effect from the steep Stabburs Valley. And the snowfall intensified. The helicopter was more or less uncontrollable for a while due to turbulence, and we started to pick up some ice. I remember telling myself, "I should never have lifted off tonight!" I asked the crew members how they felt and indicated that I wanted to continue for a mile or so and then turn back home. They understood that I was uncertain about the situation and that I was about to lose confidence in our ability to perform a safe pickup under these conditions. One by one they started to give me positive feedback. I remember the rescue swimmer said he trusted my skills and that he would go down the wire if I wanted him to! My confidence increased, and we continued. We accomplished the mission successfully.

This example indicates that the bonding of the unit and individuals' will and commitment to each other's performance had been strengthened after the integration of emotional aspects into debriefing.

Trust

Trust is another critical variable that is closely related to motivation because an environment of trust is the foundation for relationships and open feedback. It is difficult to define *trust* since it is a vague term that depends on individual perception, and literature on leadership does not contribute a blueprint of the term. Ronald Heifetz describes trust in authority relationships "as a matter of predictability along two dimensions—values and skill."[58] Roger Mayer,

James Davis, and F. David Schoorman explain trust as "the willingness of a party to be vulnerable to the actions of another party based on the expectation that the other party will perform a particular action important to the trustor, irrespective of the ability to monitor or control that other party."[59] In the holistic debriefing model, the meaning of trust is a positive expectation that another will not act opportunistically, where "opportunistically" refers to the risk and vulnerability that exist in any trusting relationship. Positive expectation means that relationships with the other party already exist and that the trust is built on earlier experiences. It takes time to build trust, and it is preserved through a continuous process. Unfortunately, trust can easily be lost if the positive expectations are not met. William Dyer states that trust is "the glue that keeps team members working together, and when trust is lost, it is very difficult to regain."[60] Ron Zemke asserts that "trust develops over time, can be dashed in an instant, and repairs very slowly."[61] In holistic debriefing, trust is the central factor in the process's success because trust provides the foundation for sufficient openness among individuals in the group. To build trust, the leader must know what generates it.

Mayer, Davis, and Schoorman assert three important leadership characteristics for creating an environment of trust: ability, benevolence, and integrity.[62] The introduction of psychological debriefing in the RNoAF's 330th and 337th Squadrons in the period 2001–2008 was internally supported by several feedback sessions in which the squadron commander together with the wing commanders tried to summarize and categorize the feedback from subordinates to define the leader's role in this type of debriefing. This feedback indicates that the leader had to be perceived as honest, interpersonally competent, loyal, and consistent before the subordinates responded with trust. Honesty is linked to integrity, and this was seen as the most critical dimension of trust. The leader's willingness and effort to establish an environment of trust within the unit is critical because it signals to the personnel that the leader believes in them and the potential of growth within the unit. This type of community building is a central factor in servant leadership based on the concept that true leadership occurs from the deep desire to serve others.[63] Nevertheless, the element of trust must go further than the leader-subordinate perspective within the unit itself.

The organizational community as a whole should ideally signal trust and caretaking as a foundational element that "runs like a red thread" through the entire RNoAF. The feedback gained from the initial introduction of psychological debriefing in the two RNoAF maritime helicopter squadrons indicates a perception among the personnel of insufficient organizational focus on these elements. As one helicopter pilot expressed during one feedback session:

> In the operational environment it always comes down to focusing on the operations—how you accomplish the mission. The RNoAF does not have a strong culture of benevolence. If you are strong and do your things right, then everything is fine. But if you make some mistakes and show uncertainty, you will lose your respect, authority, and support. So I do not feel the need to share my inner experiences and show my weaknesses outside this squadron. . . . It is difficult enough to share them with you.

This statement highlights the contradiction that exists between the dimensions of security and growth and the challenges associated with it. A sense of distrust, insecurity, or lack of organizational foundation will represent a challenge for the leader when implementing holistic debriefing within the unit. Organizational cohesion is critical because the leader must be perceived as trustworthy by the subordinates for them to give up some security for growth. If the subordinates sense a lack of support or organizational foundation, they will most likely be more skeptical and reserved. Thus, for an organization to facilitate growth, it must be able to signal coherent trust from top to bottom.

Recommendations

> *After the accident I experienced many strong emotions and difficult feelings. I wanted a confirmation . . . that I had done the right thing—but I never got it. The response I got was just, "It's good you are safe on ground. Can you fly again tomorrow?" The surroundings did not understand my emotions and experiences. I think this is very sad.*
>
> —Norwegian F-16 pilot, 2006
> Moldjord et al., *Liv og lære i operative miljøer*

After an accident, most people will experience some degree of emotional turmoil. In most situations this turmoil will disappear quickly, but in other situations it will not. The central question is always how the individual experienced the situation. What kind of emotions and thoughts did the individual have? How did the surroundings help the individual to freely express those emotions and thoughts afterwards? As mentioned earlier, emotions have a tendency to be shadowed by cognitional and behavioral aspects of the traditional military debriefing. To bring the emotions to the surface, one must establish a routine for sharing all aspects of valid experiences in the regular debriefing. This means a sufficient trust and confidence level must be established within the unit at an early stage. To be able to successfully create a debriefing concept with sufficient trust and confidence, the leader must clearly state the intentions of the holistic debriefing concept and bring it to realization through training. The RNoAF would benefit in many ways from bringing the emotional aspect to the surface.

First, airmen are valuable resources with critical professional competence that the RNoAF cannot afford to lose because of their inability to cope with accumulated stress. Second, solidarity and loyalty will be strengthened if leadership shows insight in and acknowledgement of individual needs. In other words, the practice of true servant leadership can lead to increased trust and confidence. Last, one positive spin-off effect of establishing an environment in which colleagues can share their inner feelings is strengthened unity. This is an effect that has increased in importance because of the shift in community. The family, hometown, and church have traditionally been the vital sources for community, while today our workplace is more and more becoming this vital source.[64] The RNoAF should therefore aim to build the competence and interpersonal skills necessary to build the trustful community that makes employees loyal and united. One effective way of doing this is to implement the emotional aspect into leadership through holistic debriefing and make it a regular element of daily operations.

In times of great transition and shift in community, leadership becomes the key to mission accomplishment. The leader points the way and establishes confidence in the midst of seeming chaos. Jay Conger claims that the magnitude of today's changes will demand not only more leadership but also newer forms of leadership.[65] He tells us that "the danger in any period of paradigm shift is that we will turn to our old tried-and-true ways to answer the new paradigm's demands."[66] The essence in our context is that military subordinates expect their leaders to have more interpersonal skills than before. This is partly a result of the shift in community where the employer now is expected to take responsibility for the individual's well-being and partly as a result of the desire for lifelong personal growth in the Western world. Servant leadership offers a leadership philosophy that encourages people to become more than a mere worker in an organization.[67] "With servant leadership, people grow as individuals and find meaning in and through their work."[68] The servant leader may be like a coach and teaching supervisor. Stephen Covey describes characteristics of a servant leader as being a whole person, similar to the ideal individual visualized in the Core Model.[69] These skills can be trained in supportive and constructive environments that assist in deeper learning experiences. The educational entity within the RNoAF can represent such an environment because the setting is operationally safe and there is room for failure. But the critical transition back to the operational environment has traditionally not safeguarded the leader's newly learned skills.

Coaching is critically important, and it should not end the moment the participants leave the classroom. Active and persistent coaching must be a continuous activity for new leadership skills to take hold. It is therefore important that leaders in the RNoAF are not only given the opportunity but also are enrolled in a mandatory coaching program. Continual contact and follow-up support through coaching is the key to success when bringing the emotional aspect of leadership into play at the operational level. Further support and coaching for leaders can take place by creating three- or four-person teams of peers. The idea is that these leaders learn from each other in "a mutual support system with encouragement, wisdom, and truth."[70]

Conclusion

The reason for incorporating holistic debriefing in the RNoAF is to increase mission effectiveness. By integrating the emotional aspect into the traditional debriefing, the leader can establish a more holistic arena for learning that covers all essential aspects of individual growth and development: behavioral, cognitive, and emotional. This is important for individuals, units, and organizations because emotions that were experienced before, during, or after the mission may have an impact on operational effectiveness. The leader is responsible for mission effectiveness, and for holistic debriefing to be successful the leader is the key. Hence, the practice of holistic debriefing has to be adopted as a standardized concept throughout the organization to be fully integrated in the RNoAF. Knowledge of essential elements for human growth and development must be integrated in the leadership training at educational entities throughout the RNoAF. This should include basic understanding of individual needs and tendencies, motivation, and trust.

This study has shown how theory relates to practice by exploring some of the positive effects experienced after integrating emotional aspects into the traditional debriefing at the RNoAF's maritime helicopter squadrons. It is difficult to objectively measure how the integration of emotional aspects into the traditional debriefing has affected mission effectiveness. However, the use of a holistic approach indicates that the working environment has improved due to increased trust and confidence, better interpersonal exchange of information, and increased individual self-knowledge. The assumption is that these variables are important for mitigating the negative effects of stress. Hence, stress can be kept below a threatening level and thereby improve overall mission performance. Literature on the theme supports these assumptions.

The positive effects of a holistic approach in leadership through debriefing create a hope for the RNoAF's future as an attractive employer and a professional producer of airpower. The community is in many ways going through a paradigm shift in that personnel now expect the RNoAF to take more responsibility for their well-being and lifelong personal growth. The holistic approach in the practice of leadership is an important step for the RNoAF to achieve exactly that, and the holistic debriefing described in this paper can be a valuable tool.

Notes

(All notes appear in shortened form. For full details, see the appropriate entry in the bibliography.)

1. Bass, "From Transactional to Transformational Leadership," 19–31.
2. Bjartveit and Kjærstad, *Fra kaos til kosmos*, 17.
3. Bruner, *Actual Minds*, 111.
4. Ibid., 61.
5. Solberg, *Krisehaandtering—Emosjonell Debriefing*, 1–2.
6. Moldjord et al., *Liv og lære i operative miljøer*, 390.
7. Chief of the Norwegian Defence Staff, *Forsvarssjefens grunnsyn på ledelse i Forsvaret*.
8. Ibid.
9. Royal Norwegian Air Force, *Håndbok i lederskap for Luftforsvaret*, 348.
10. Chief of the Norwegian Defence Staff, *Forsvarssjefens grunnsyn på ledelse i Forsvaret*, 1–3.
11. Conger, "Brave New World," 46.
12. Moldjord et al., *Liv og lære i operative miljøer*, 11.
13. Bruner, *Actual Minds*, 69.
14. Ibid.
15. Ibid.
16. Ibid., 117.
17. Ibid., 118.
18. Atkinson et al., *Introduction to Psychology*, 417.
19. Fromm, *Man for Himself*, 45.
20. Moxnes, *Hverdagens Angst*, 33.
21. Bjartveit and Kjærstad, *Fra kaos til kosmos*, 22–23.
22. Moxnes, *Hverdagens Angst*, 194.
23. Bjartveit and Kjærstad, *Fra kaos til kosmos*, 17.
24. Useem, *Leadership Moment*, 60.
25. Ibid., 59.
26. Moxnes, *Hverdagens Angst*, 48.
27. Kierkegaard, *Fear and Trembling*, 30.
28. Aldwin, *Stress, Coping, and Development*, 79.
29. Maslow, *Motivation and Personality*, 77–97.
30. Ibid., 273.
31. Moxnes, *Hverdagens Angst*, 46.
32. Ibid., 47.
33. Ibid., 46.
34. Ibid., 47, 49.
35. Moldjord et al., *Liv og lære i operative miljøer*, 11.
36. Burnette, "Suicide Rates."
37. Moxnes, *Hverdagens Angst*, 52.

38. Bjørvik, *Arbeids-og lederpsykologi*, 132.
39. Ibid., 133.
40. Moxnes, *Hverdagens Angst*, 78.
41. Higgins, "Self-Discrepancy," 319–40.
42. Winnicott, *Maturational Process*, 140–52; Nyeng, *Det autentiske menneske*; Pierrakos, *Core Energetics*; Monsen, *Det elskende menneske*; and Moldjord et al., *Liv og lære i operative miljøer*, 373.
43. Higgins, "Self-Discrepancy," 319–40.
44. Moldjord et al., *Liv og lære i operative miljøer*, 370.
45. Ibid., 369.
46. Bowlby, *Secure Base*, 1–38.
47. Higgins, "Self-Discrepancy," 319–40.
48. Moldjord et al., *Liv og lære i operative miljøer*, 373.
49. Solberg, *Krisehaandtering—Emosjonell Debriefing*.
50. Hytten and Ursin, "Outcome Expectancies," 171–84.
51. Retterstøl and Weisæth, *Katastrofer og kriser*, 67.
52. Ibid.
53. Christianson, *Traumatiska minnen*, 48.
54. Allport, *Personality*, 48.
55. Wheatley, *Leadership and the New Science*, 145.
56. Stueland, "Mental oppfølging etter hendelser," 48.
57. Ibid., 31.
58. Heifetz, *Leadership without Easy Answers*, 107.
59. Mayer, Davis, and Schoorman, "Integrative Model of Organizational Trust," 712.
60. Dyer, *Team Building*, 22.
61. Zemke, "Can You Manage Trust?" 77.
62. Mayer, Davis, and Schoorman, "Integrative Model of Organizational Trust," 714.
63. Greenleaf, *Servant Leadership*.
64. Conger, "Brave New World," 49.
65. Ibid., 46.
66. Ibid., 47.
67. Ruschman, "Servant-Leadership."
68. Landry, "Servant Leadership," 219.
69. Covey, *8th Habit*, 21.
70. Conger, "Brave New World," 56.

Bibliography

Aldwin, C. *Stress, Coping, and Development: An Integrative Approach.* New York: The Guilford Press, 1994.

Allport, G. *Personality: A Psychological Interpretation.* New York: Reinhart & Winston, 1937.

Atkinson, R. L., R. C. Atkinson, E. E. Smith, and E. R. Hilgard. *Introduction to Psychology.* 9th ed. Orlando, FL: Harcourt Brace Jovanovich, 1987.

Bass, Bernard. "From Transactional to Transformational Leadership." *Organizational Dynamics* 18, no. 3 (Winter 1990): 19–31.

Bjartveit, S., and T. Kjærstad. *Fra kaos til kosmos.* Oslo, Norway: Oslo Kolle Forlag, 1996.

Bjørvik, K. J. *Arbeids-og lederpsykologi, 3. utgave.* Oslo, Norway: Bedriftsøkonomisk Forlag, 1987.

Bowlby, J. *A Secure Base: Clinical Applications of Attachment Theory.* Bristol, UK: J. W. Arrowsmith, 1988.

Bruner, J. *Actual Minds, Possible Words.* Cambridge, MA: Harvard University Press, 1986.

Burnette, A. "Suicide Rates at All-Time High among Active-Duty Soldiers." *The Science behind Today's News*, 5 February 2008. Science in the Headlines. The National Academies Office of News and Public Information. http://www.nationalacademies.org/headlines/20080205.html.

Chaudron, D. "Avoid the Training Hammer When Implementing Change." *Organized Change Consultancy*, 2008. http://organizedchange.com/trainham.htm.

Chief of the Norwegian Defence Staff. *Forsvarssjefens grunnsyn på ledelse i Forsvaret* [The Approach to Leadership in the Armed Forces]. Oslo, Norway: FO/P&I, 1992.

Christianson, S. Å. *Traumatiska minnen.* Stockholm, Sweden: Bokførlaget Natur og Kultur, 1994.

Conger, J. A. "The Brave New World of Leadership Training." *Organizational Dynamics* 21, no. 3 (Winter 1993): 46–58.

Covey, S. R. *The 8th Habit: From Effectiveness to Greatness.* New York: Simon & Schuster, Inc., 2004.

Dyer, W. G. *Team Building: Current Issues and New Alternatives.* Reading, MA: Addison-Wesley Publishing Company, 1995.

Fromm, E. *Man for Himself: An Inquiry into the Psychology of Ethics*. New York: Rhinehart & Co, Inc., 1947.

Greenleaf, R. K. *Servant Leadership: A Journey into the Nature of Legitimate Power and Greatness*. Mahwah, NJ: Pulist, 2002.

Heifetz, R. *Leadership without Easy Answers*. Cambridge, MA: The Belknap Press of Harvard University Press, 1994.

Higgins, E. Tory. "Self-Discrepancy: A Theory Relating Self and Affect." *Psychological Review* 94, no. 3 (July 1987): 319–40.

Hytten, K., and H. Ursin. "Outcome Expectancies and Psychosomatic Consequences." In *Personal Coping: Theory, Research, and Application*, edited by B. N. Carpenter, 171–84. Westport, CT: Praeger/Greenwood, 1992.

Kierkegaard, S. *Fear and Trembling*. Princeton, NJ: Princeton University Press, 1941.

Landry, B. W. "Servant Leadership, Building of Community, and POWs." *International Journal of Servant Leadership* 4, no. 1 (2008): 217–32.

Maslow, A. *Motivation and Personality*. New York: Harper, 1964.

Mayer, R. C., J. H. Davis, and F. D. Schoorman. "An Integrative Model of Organizational Trust." *Academy of Management Review* 20, no. 3 (1995): 709–34.

Moldjord, C., A. Arntzen, K. Firing, O. A. Solberg, and J. C. Laberg. *Liv og lære i operative miljøer. Tøffe menn grater!* Bergen, Norway: Fagbokforlaget, 2007.

Monsen, Nina Karin. *Det elskende menneske* [The Loving Human]. Oslo, Norway: Universitetsforlaget, 1987.

Moxnes, P. *Hverdagens Angst*. Vol. 3, *Utgave*. Oslo, Norway: Forlaget Paul Moxnes, 1995.

Nyeng, F. *Det autentiske mennekse—med Charles Taylors blikk på menneksevitenskap og moral* [The Authentically Human—with Charles Taylor's View on Human Science and Morale]. Oslo, Norway: Fagbokforlaget, 2000.

Pierrakos, J. C. *Core Energetics: Developing the Capacity to Love and Heal*. Mendicino, CA: LifeRythms, 1987.

Retterstøl, N., and L. Weisæth. *Katastrofer og kriser*. Oslo, Norway: Universitetsforlaget, 1985.

Royal Norwegian Air Force. *Håndbok i lederskap for Luftforsvaret* [Handbook in Leadership for the RNoAF]. Oslo, Norway: FO/P&I, 1995.

Ruschman, N. L. "Servant-Leadership and the Best Companies to Work for in America." In *Focus on Leadership: Servant-Leadership for the 21st Century*, edited by L. C. Spears and M. Lawrence, 123–40. New York: John Wiley & Sons, 2002.

Solberg, O. A. *Krisehaandtering—Emosjonell Debriefing* [Emotional Debriefing]. A compendium at Norwegian Air War Academy. Trondheim, Norway: Luftkrigsskolen, 1997.

Stueland, E. "Mental oppfølging etter hendelser [Mental Follow-Up after Incidents]—en mangelvare i dagens Luftforsvar?" Postgraduate thesis, Norwegian Air War Academy, Trondheim, Norway, 2006.

Useem, M. *The Leadership Moment: Nine True Stories of Triumph and Disaster and Their Lessons for Us All*. New York: Three Rivers Press, 1998.

Wheatley, M. J. *Leadership and the New Science: Discovering Order in a Chaotic World*. San Francisco, CA: Berret-Koehler Publishers, Inc., 2006.

Winnicott, D. W. *The Maturational Process and the Facilitating Environment: Studies in the Theory of Emotional Development*. New York: International UP Inc., 1965.

Zemke, R. "Can You Manage Trust?" *Training* 37, no. 2 (February 2000): 76–81.

www.ingramcontent.com/pod-product-compliance
Lightning Source LLC
Chambersburg PA
CBHW071016200526
45171CB00007B/277